Live a Full Life *of* Inspiration *&* Devotion

Live a Full Life of Inspiration & Devotion

Todd Hansen

Acclaim Press
MORLEY, MISSOURI

Acclaim Press
— Your Next Great Book —
P.O. Box 238
Morley, MO 63767
(573) 472-9800
www.acclaimpress.com

Book Design: Steward & Wise Graphic Design
Cover Design: M. Frene Melton

ISBN: 978-1-942613-82-4 | 1-942613-82-2
Library of Congress Control Number: 2017916140

First Printing: 2017
Printed in the United States of America
10 9 8 7 6 5 4 3 2 1

This publication was produced using available information.
The publisher regrets it cannot assume responsibility for errors or omissions.

Contents

Foreword 7
Dedication 10
This Book Is For 11
Everyone Has a Story 15
Am I the Only One? 23
Find the Lord *Before* You Need Him 29
All That Really Matters 35
Where They Should Not Have Been 39
Where They Should Not Have Stayed 41
Always Ask God 45
We *Are* Healed 49
Have You Done *All* You Can, or
Are You Serious With Your Prayers? 51
God's Economy 57
God Has a Plan 65
Don't Be a Settler 67
Change Equals Growth 73
Whatever Your Circumstances,
You Can Be a Blessing 75
Have It Your Way 79
Visions of Heaven 83
Clean Out the Clutter 87
The Turtle, the Opossum, and Abraham 91
The Least of These 95
Look Ahead, Not Behind 97
Retreat Doesn't Equal Surrender 99
In Conclusion 103
About the Author 107
Scriptural References 108
Biblical Characters & Terms 110
Index 111

Foreword

Starting something always seems to be the hardest. As when you are building a building, the first row of blocks or vinyl siding has to be straight and level or the rest will be doomed to follow the same incorrect pattern. Therefore, you feel the same amount of pressure when you sit down and start to write. You can struggle for days to find just the right word or phrase to get started, to grab the reader's attention, and to make him or her want to read what you have committed to paper. So, here I sit about to embark on the journey of my life—I am going to write a book. Does that make me a writer? First of all, I don't feel qualified. I feel fear that I don't have the talent to see the job to completion. Secondly, this is not just a novel or a work of fiction; it will also be labeled as inspirational. Do I have the power to inspire? I have the answer to that question—no, I don't, but it's not about me. I know in my own strength that I do not have all the answers. And I could tell myself that I should wait until everything is just right, until I have *all* the answers, until I can live out a perfect example. But I know that will never happen; there is only one that is perfect, and He is the inspiration for my writing. So, yes, I feel this is a calling, something that I feel led and called to do. My hope is that, as you read, you will be encouraged and inspired, not by me but by the one I point you to. For as it says in the book of 1st Samuel 30:6, *"and David was greatly distressed; for the people spake of stoning him, because the soul of all the people was grieved, every man for his sons and for his daughters: but David encouraged himself in the Lord his God."* I want this book to be an encouragement to the readers and to encourage them also to be an encouragement to others by going out and sharing the Gospel. There may be a time when you have no one else to turn to, but you, as David did, can encourage yourself in the Lord. And I hope this book helps and inspires you to do just that.

Part Two

Well, this book has been hanging out in the digital world unfinished for several years now, and the time has come for it to be finished. I hope now that I am older, that I am also wiser, and the completed product will be better. When I first thought about finishing this book, my assumption was that I would edit what I had started, but I have decided to leave it as is for now, with the exception of this addition to the foreword. When I started on this project, I was just beginning as a writer; since then, I have written a weekly inspirational column in a few newspapers, as well as online, for a few years and spent some time working at a small newspaper. But my writing career came to a halt when I enrolled in college in my mid-forties. I have since completed my MBA and now have begun to write once more. All the chapters can be read independently, but hopefully, they will share a common thread. I hope you enjoy and are truly inspired.

Dedication

I would like to dedicate this book to my parents and grandparents—Max and Juanita Hansen and JW and Mary Lue Hansen—for without them it would not have been possible. Without them I might not have been raised in a loving Christian home and been instilled with Christian values.

My only regret is that none of them lived to see this day.

This picture of them is one of my favorites. It was taken on mom and dad's wedding day.

This Book Is For...

This book is not for the lost, but for the broken. Of course, I hope someone reads this book and finds Jesus, but realistically my hope is for it to be an encouragement for those who are already Christians. I trust that the principles taught in this book will help to heal the broken and break the chains of those bound by religious traditions and the opinions of multitudes.

Live a Full Life *of* Inspiration *&* Devotion

Everyone Has a Story

I'd like to take a little time in this chapter to give you a little more background on me and the subject matter for this book. Maybe we could call it the foreword part three. For those of you who are familiar with my writing, you know that I have a weekly column in a few local newspapers, but maybe by the time this is published, my column may be nationally syndicated and I may be a household name. But I'm not holding my breath just yet. Anyway, what I am trying to do is to take some of my columns that I felt like were inspiring but didn't feel like I did the subject justice in a few words and expound on those. So, in a sense, this will be a collection of short essays. One would then think that one chapter would have no connection to the other, so if you choose, you could jump around reading where ever the book opened. Well, that's a good thought, but it is my intent to weave some fabric throughout the collection to set one story up for the next. But I haven't finished the book yet, so I don't really know how it will be. Now sit down, hang on, and we will see where this adventure takes us.

Most of my adult life I have tried to serve God however I possibly could. I have tried several forms of ministry: singing, preaching, radio broadcast, and all forms of church-related activities. But most of all, I love to sing. So, you say, then why are you trying to write a book? Well, I'm kind of wondering that myself. Well, I've found that you can't always do what you want to do or maybe what you think that you are good at, but you must follow the Lord's direction and go through the doors that he opens. As I mentioned earlier, I have tried to become involved with many different forms and types of ministry, but the one that's seems to be the most fruitful is my newspaper column. In the past, professionally, I have felt that I could communicate better with "pen and ink" or, in reality, a computer than I could with the spoken word. So, that's why I have chosen to take it to the next level and write a book.

Like the title of this chapter, everyone has a story, and that's a little bit of mine. As you read through the pages, you will notice that I tend not to use real names or places or tell the stories of real people. I guess you could think that I just didn't want to do the legwork to get permission or to write up all the footnotes. But the truth is that the names are not that important because, like I say, everyone's got a story. Some may say that the devil is in the details, but the truth is that the point of every story goes way beyond the individuals themselves. I want to show a higher purpose and to inspire us all to live up to the purpose that God has for each of us. So, with that all said, let us move on to the topic of the chapter, and this chapter I might note is a new topic and not something that I am revising, but who knows, by the time you read this book, I may publish the short version of this as a column.

I just cannot seem to get started without stopping and giving you more background on how I think, or better stated, my worldview. For most of my adult life, I have attended a very conservative church. But conservative or liberal is like beauty—it's in the eye of the beholder. So, anyway, I guess some would say that I have led a sheltered life. But, you know, I guess it has always been the crowd I'm in that has determined my status. But I'm not saying that in a bad way; no, I'm not one for following the crowd. What I guess I mean is that many times in a church situation, I have been one of the most liberal in the congregation, but then when I would go to work, I would be, by far, the most conservative. Do I have you confused yet? If not, maybe you have been there, too. Or maybe at least I've given you an idea of how conservative some of the churches I've been in were. So, I guess maybe I have lived a sheltered life. But I never thought so, until I thought I had seen everything. I was 43 years old; I had worked for a major corporation; I had traveled, both personally and professionally; and I had even been overseas (well, at least in the Caribbean). No, I didn't think at all that I'd lived a sheltered life, until I got a dose of the real world. And, no, I don't mean the TV show. How can they put people up in a fancy location and care for their almost every need and call it the "real world" any way? Oh, but I digress. And you will find out as you read my writing that we will "rabbit hunt" a lot. That may be why I can communicate better on paper than verbally because, when I write, I have the chance to go back and edit. Well, how can I make a long story short? I seem to be best at making a short story long. Anyway, in the middle of a time in my life which I was searching for a new direction, I found myself in an environment like I had never been before. Well, as I sit here typing away at the little keys I'm thinking that this may end up as a comedy rather than inspirational. But isn't that just like real life, anyway? I'm also searching my mind for words that can describe people with a different worldview without sounding condescending or insulting. But maybe that's the point; everyone's got a story, don't they? One must be open-minded and realize that just because people are different doesn't mean that they are automatically wrong. It just means that maybe they have a different background and have not seen the world the way you have. Boy, that doesn't sound like something a person that is socially and politically conservative would say, does it? But let's go back a couple of rabbit trails. In the past, for the most part, I was only around people at church or at work. My interactions with people at functions other than that were few and far between. Did I mention that I'm a recovering workaholic? And the people that I worked with, even the ones that were not Christians, were socially conservative, so we had some common ground we could fit in. And apart from church and work, when I went to a ball game or to the corner store, we lived in a small

So, at times we must endure for a while for His greater good and to seek to fulfill His purpose in our lives.

town, and everyone still, for the most part, shared those "small hometown values." So, at a time in my life when I was looking for a change, boy, did I find one. I once told someone at the factory that it was like "Egypt" for me, although I don't believe he understood the biblical reference. Because it was a place that I needed deliverance from and God wouldn't have to tell me twice it was time to go. But at the same time I understood that just like in Egypt, as God was growing his people as a nation and building them up, you have to realize that there is a purpose in every situation. That is, if you believe in God and seek to follow His direction. So, at times we must endure for a while for His greater good and to seek to fulfill His purpose in our lives. Depending on your circumstances, that might be hard to take, but everyone has a story, don't they? Well, it just might be that I couldn't have written this book if it wasn't for that experience, but the story isn't over yet.

Well, even though it is almost anticlimactic and unnecessary now, I'll finish the direction I was on before I got so sidetracked. I found myself working with a group of people oh so much different than I had experienced before. For one thing, I was in a situation where being a white male over forty was in a minority class. I don't want you for a minute to think that my life is swayed by prejudice of any kind—we have hosted and worked with exchange students from many countries, and I love all God's people. It is just that some I have not been around as much as others have. I came in contact with people who would confess sins openly in the break room that would make a sailor blush or at least I thought so. Most of the people would almost braggingly tell of jailhouse adventures and things that I thought no one would talk about in public, at least not admit that you did them. I have always thought that the people on those reality and TV talk shows were actors and made up most of that stuff, until now. They told me that I didn't fit in because I had never served any jail time or had a tattoo. Someone there even offered to do a tattoo for me, but I kindly rejected the offer, no body parts pierced, either. But I came to realize that, but for the grace of almighty God, I could have been as one of them. Had I not been raised in a loving, church going family, had someone not shared the gospel with me, I could have been caught up in a life of crime and drugs. I could have been one of them like in the book of Mark 6:34: *"And Jesus, when he came out, saw much people, and was moved with compassion toward them, because they were as sheep not having a shepherd: and he began to teach them many things."* Thank God that he has been my shepherd, and this is why I write because as it says in Romans 10:14: *"How then shall they call on him in whom they have not believed? And how shall they believe in him of whom they have not heard? And how shall they hear without a preacher?"* So, to all I can, I want to be that shepherd, that preacher, that teacher, that one who inspires you and causes you to turn to God as the source of your encouragement and inspiration. Because everyone has a story, don't they? And maybe there is still time for some of them to have a happier ending.

Am I the Only One?

Have you ever thought, am I the only one serving God? It is amazing in this great big world how we can get such "tunnel vision" to think that way. But I'm sure that thought has crossed the mind of every Christian at some point in their life. I believe that one of the greatest examples of this is in 1 Kings 19. Here, we read a story of the great Prophet Elijah expressing those very same emotions. Is it not great to get these insights from the Bible on these great men, to see how they have low points just like us? I've heard some say that it proves the Bible to be true because if someone was going to make it all up, they would sure leave out all the bad parts and all the moral failure in the lives of the great men and women of the Bible. I believe that the reason these stories are included are to tell the whole story, the "whole truth," if you will. But we must view all things in moderation; let us not wallow in the fact that even the great ones can have a slip or a bad day. But let us take the approach that we can all—yes, I said "all"—do great things for God if we put our heart to it. As we read in verse 10, Elijah tells the Lord "and I, even I only, am left; and they seek my life, to take it away." Haven't we all felt that way at times? Like we are the only ones, and everyone else is out to get us? But let's not get carried away and take this out of the whole context of 1 Kings.

... if the Lord God Jehovah be God, then him you must serve.

Let us go back just one page, back just one chapter. For if we read the eighteenth chapter, you see great victory in his life, for it is here that we read of a great "show down." Just like a story from the legends of the nineteenth century-American West. I know some of you are bound to be John Wayne fans. When I read the 1 Kings 18, that's just what it makes me think of, a scene from an old Western movie in which the hero calls out the bad guys to gunfight at high noon. But in this true story, Elijah challenges not just one but 450 prophets of Baal. And in the common language of our time, he tells them to "put up or shut up." He says for too long the people of Israel have been uncertain on whom the real God was and who they should serve. So, Elijah then issues the challenge to the people and to the prophets of Baal: if

Baal be god, then serve him, but if the Lord God Jehovah be God, then him you must serve. So, to circle the wagons a bit and draw this story in some, Elijah suggested that they each sacrifice a bull on a wooden altar and that they would call on God and on Baal, and the true God would answer with fire. So, being a gentleman, Elijah gave the prophets of Baal the first chance. So, they proceeded to dance and chant and do all manners of things, but in the end, no fire. So, now its Elijah's turn, and to make things more difficult, so no one could say he got lucky, he had his altar watered down. Not once but three times. And, yes, in the end Jehovah proves to be the true God of Israel and the people turn back to him and kill the prophets of Baal with the sword. So, he should be on cloud nine, walking in tall cotton, or any other cliché that you want to use. But then he falls to desperation after Queen Jezebel threatens his life. Now get a

... Satan is the most worried about us is when we are the closest to God and when we are doing His will.

grip on this: Elijah has just won the showdown with 450 prophets and now he is put to flight by one evil queen. That, sports fans, is the most important part of this story. He didn't have a series of bad days and then decide that the world was coming to an end and he was the only one serving God. It was at a time when he was on the top of his game, when he had just charged Hell with a water pistol. You say why? Why? Tell us why. Well, if I had the answers to that question, I would have started writing best sellers a long time ago. But I do know that when Satan is the most worried about us is when we are the closest to God and when we are doing His will. That is when Satan just has to jump up and get in our stuff, so to speak, to get us off our game, so he can defeat us. When you're setting under a shade tree watching the world go by and only thinking of yourself, you're not causing Satan any trouble, but when you go and show up 450 of his guys, well, that's a different story. In 1 Kings 19:7–16, the Lord ministers to and encourages Elijah and caps it off with this statement in verse 18: *"Yet I have left me seven thousand in Israel, all the knees which have not bowed unto Baal, and every mouth which hath not kissed him."* That brings us to another question, where were those 7,000 when Elijah needed some help and encouragement and show of support?

Earlier this year (this passage was written in 2006) because of some statements of faith I made in leaving a former job, I was encouraged by the faith of others. And I learned that several of my distant coworkers were Christians, but I didn't know it until then. Because I opened the door, so to speak, they shared stories of their faith and their ministry activities. Why are we so slow to share our Christian testimony? Others around us could benefit so much from our faith in Christ if we would just stand up and let the world know where we stand. It seems that there are millions of Christians in America today, but

... get out and be a witness for the good that Christ has done ...

many seem to be in the "secret service." It is time that the Christians get out of the Army Reserve and step out on the front lines and make a difference in this country. Yes, I know that standing up for Christ sometimes comes with a cost, but Matthew 5:10 says *"Blessed are they which are persecuted for righteousness' sake: for theirs is the kingdom of heaven."* And later in the chapter Jesus goes on to say in verse 16, *"Let your light so shine before men, that they may see your good works, and glorify your Father which is in heaven."* So, let's all make it a point to get out and be a witness for the good that Christ has done for us. Not only to be a witness for the lost but also, just as importantly to be an encouragement to other believers. To sum things up, I'm writing this to be an inspiration, not only to just make us feel good as we read and sit in our nice warm living rooms but also to inspire you to inspire others. There are some "Elijahs" out there who think they are the only ones, while there are 7,000 of you sitting on the couch, waiting for someone else to go encourage them. After a statement like that is when my pastor would say, "I'm preachin' a lot better than y'all are shoutin'." And that's hard to write, and it's hard to live, but the fact of the matter is that it is the truth. Winning the lost is not a one man job. Billy Graham is a great man, but he couldn't do it on his own. Maybe you don't feel like you are good at personal outreach, but maybe you can go with someone who is. You might not be a singer or a preacher, but I bet you know several that you can pray for. I think you get the picture I am trying to portray; I am trying, as I said, to inspire you to inspire others, so as a team, we can get the job done. Because remember the ones I mentioned in chapter one? They all have a story, and they need some help before it's too late. I can't reach them all, or maybe I can't even reach any of them, but maybe, just maybe, you can.

Find the Lord Before You Need Him

As you probably know, I am a gospel singer. As I say that, it reminds me of another rabbit trail, but to shorten it: what you do for a living does not define you. You need to define yourself in God's purpose, not in man's, so when I joined Facebook ten years behind everyone else, that was one of the questions it asked, and, thus, I answered gospel singer. I will go on about that later, but to this point, there is a song I have sung for several years that contains a line that I love: "Find the Lord before you need him." I just love that. I started not to write whose song it is, but just to let you know that God can use anything or anybody, it is a Randy Travis song. It was written by Kim Tribble, but Randy recorded it on his gospel album. Who knows what his condition will be by the time you read this, but his life has had more ups and downs, mostly downs, than a roller coaster the last few years. But enough of that. I like the song "Don't Ever Sell Your Saddle," and I love that particular line.

Do not raise your hand or laugh out loud, but we all know someone who only comes to church when they are in trouble. Reaching out from there, many who never come to church try to get help from the Church or individual Christians when they are in a tight spot. We can all name a few who are in church every time the doors are open when they are out of a job or when their marriage is in trouble, but when the storm passes, then even Pinkerton couldn't find

How can you call out to someone you don't even know?

them. Yes, we all know a few of them, but the ones I'm thinking about are not even saved—they have never accepted Christ, so they don't know him. How can you call out to someone you don't even know? A few years ago, Carrie Underwood got everyone's attention with "Jesus Take the Wheel." While it was a cute song, it is not good theology for everyone. As I said, how can you call out to someone you don't even know? Yes, the "Jesus take the wheel" prayer might work for a Christian, but what about a lost person? All my life I have prayed for everyone, prayed for every need they presented. However, up until recently, I never gave any thought to their spiritual condition in regards to prayer for their needs. I just knew my God could do all things. He told us to pray, so I prayed. Lately I have come to realize, just as I have always known, that the only sinner's prayer God hears is for salvation; otherwise, He never acknowledges. So then why do we pray for the needs of sinners and expect God to fix it? What right or promise do they have to expect God to move on their behalf? Have you ever thought that the problem they are in might be the device God is using to bring them around? Now, do not get all huffy and think I am saying we should not pray for sinners. That is not what I am saying, but maybe the content of our prayers should be addressed more toward their salvation than their current problem.

Back to the song, the point is we need to find God before we need Him and build that relationship with Him so that when we are in need, He will be there for us as a guide and comfort when we call. Yes, God will take care of His people. I will expound on that in a later chapter entitled "God's Economy."

> *I just knew my God could do all things. He told us to pray, so I prayed.*

But as I say *His* people. Those in the world who have never accepted Christ are not His people, so let us get first things first.

One thing most don't think about is that if you are His, you need to act like it and you need to try your best to make good decisions on the front end so that He doesn't have as much mess to clean up when things go sideways. One example of this could be something that happened to us on a recent trip to Texas. We were going to visit our daughter and her family and were driving a new-to-us-but-used vehicle, which we had just traded for a few days before. Driving along, the low tire light came on, the same one that had been on twice in a week, so I am thinking that this is not just a coincidence or just caused by cold weather. Since this was on a Friday, with Christmas just two days away, I decided that it was time to take action before it was too late. We were a few miles

Don't you think that many of the problems unbelievers face are the results of the choices and decisions that they make?

from the next large town, and my wife, with the help of Google, found a place that should be able to get us in and out of quickly. There is more to the story and I will finish it, but the point I want to make is that I did not wait until I was on the side of the road with two blown tires on Christmas Day to ask God for help. You say I'm exaggerating, but am I? Have you ever put something off, thinking it will be okay or you'll fix it later? Don't you think that many of the problems unbelievers face are the results of the choices and decisions that they make? On the other hand, you might be thinking, "Why do I need to talk to God about getting my tire fixed?" I don't want anyone to think that I'm "Super Christian," but I talk to God about everything, even the small stuff, because if you think about it, it is all small stuff to Him.

Most writers do not give free advertisements, but in this case, I will mention the place we stopped. We pulled into the quick service department of Elliott Ford in Mt. Pleasant, Texas, and they were quick to greet us and move our SUV into the garage. After about thirty minutes or so of enjoying coffee and doughnuts in their fine waiting room, one of the guys tells us we were ready. Now if you have ever had any experience with car dealerships, you can imagine that I expected to pay a high price. I was even prepared in my mind for them to come back and say that the tires couldn't be repaired and would need to be replaced, who knows, maybe even a whole new set. Thanks to God, we were blessed and surprised to find all we owed was a handshake and a Merry Christmas. Some might call that a small Christmas miracle in the times we live in. As I say, God takes care of His people. God will bless you if you will allow Him. By allowing Him, I mean that you need to ask for not only His help but also for His direction and guidance.

To sum it up first, we must find the Lord and develop a relationship with him. We need to pray, which is just talking to God. He wants to hear from us. Thirdly, we need to obey Him, we need to follow his guidance through prayer and the reading of His word. Lastly, if we follow that outline, we will be blessed.

All That Really Matters

Just a short time before I sat down to write this, I heard a song on the radio where the singer was telling of the many regrets in his life. I think it was a country song, if you could imagine sad lyrics in a country song. Anyway, before we go down that rabbit trail, I am sure we all have things in life that we wish we had done differently. Now that I'm middle-aged, I could sit all day if I let myself and look over my life and see things that I could have done differently, but enough of that—let's move on.

Just a few days ago, I read an obituary, a habit I picked up while in the newspaper business, and it was for a friend of mine from about thirty years ago. That was a time in my life when I was not living as I should have been. That is not the story for the day, but I thought about my friend; he died in an accident, unexpectedly. My thoughts drifted to the condition of his soul. I wondered if he knew Jesus. I thought about the fact that I haven't seen him in many years, and when we were friends, I don't recall if I shared the Gospel with him or not. And if I did, I wouldn't have been a credible witness of the power of God to change lives at that time.

Nevertheless, back to the beginning, while we do not need to continually repeat our same mistakes, we cannot let our lives slip into paralysis of analysis. For then we cannot accomplish anything. But on the other extreme, we can't let pride for the good things we've done overcome us, either, for as Paul says in Philippians 3: 7–8, *"But whatever things were gain to me, those I counted loss for Christ. But no, rather, I also count all things to be loss for the excellency of the knowledge of Christ Jesus my Lord, for whose sake I have suffered the loss of all things, and count them to be dung, so that I may win Christ."*

> *Just two things have lasting and eternal value: Did you commit your life and hope to Jesus? And did you tell others about his love?*

Whatever good or bad I have done is not the important things when it comes to eternity. I love the words of a Jeff and Sheri Easter song from a few years back: "all that really matters, when it's all said and done . . . when your time to go has come, is did you know Jesus, and show him to anyone."

Just two things have lasting and eternal value: Did you commit your life and hope to Jesus? And did you tell others about his love? I just told you of someone

Jesus died to pay for your sin and to give you the gift of salvation and eternal life. Trust Him today.

that may have died without me having the chance to share the Gospel with him; I can't let you be another. Jesus died to pay for your sin and to give you the gift of salvation and eternal life. Trust Him today.

That's not all I have to say about that song. For it just so happens that I recited parts of that song at my dad's funeral. For in the first verse of the song, the setting is a funeral. I'm sure you haven't heard many inspiring songs written about a funeral, but leave it to Jeff and Sheri to find one. In the song, it is stated that no one talked about material possessions but just the deceased man's love for his family and his Lord. When preparing for dad's funeral, this song came to mind because his life fit the song. He knew Jesus, and he lived it. Not just on Sunday but on every day, and those around him could tell. Was he a perfect Christian? No, no one is, but he lived his relationship with

God, day in, day out, for all the world to see, and in the end, he could be judged by this song, for all that knew him realized that he knew Jesus because of the way he lived and interacted with everyone.

This could be your story. Today could be the first day of the rest of your life, your new life as a servant of Christ. Oh, you may be saved—I'm not questioning that—but are you living to the fullest potential in your service to God? And as everyone says, I'm not talking about Christian leadership in ministry; I'm talking about daily living so that your neighbor doesn't have to wonder if you are a Christian. It is not your pastor's job to lead everyone to Christ. He is here to be a teacher and leader to encourage and train the members, so we can go out and reach people and bring them in. Sometimes it just takes a good example to lead people to Christ. Can you be that example? What will they say about you when the time comes? Will they talk about your possessions or just say he loved Jesus and everyone knew it? That story isn't written yet. You still have time to make some edits if you need to because everyone has a story, don't they?

Where They Should Not Have Been

The truth seems stranger than fiction. Sometimes you just see stuff that is so funny and strange that you just could not make it up. Like the other day while driving through Paducah, Kentucky, I happened to look up and saw a squirrel going across one of the utility lines across four lanes of traffic. No, it is not unusual to see a squirrel on a wire, but what makes this different was the bird that seemed to be attacking him. Of course, I do not know why, but this bird was flying around this squirrel, seemingly trying his best to cause him to fall. It made me think how Satan waits until we have our hands full and then attacks.

1 Peter 5:8 says, *"Be sober, be vigilant; because your adversary the devil walks about like a roaring lion, seeking whom he may devour."* That bird may not seem much like a lion to you, but to that squirrel, he could be very threatening, with the real threat being the hard pavement over twenty feet below. Peter goes on

to say in verse 9, *"Resist him, steadfast in the faith, knowing that the same sufferings are experienced by your brotherhood in the world."* Just as the squirrel had to try his best to ignore the bird and hold on and keep going, we have to resist Satan when he comes against us.

Most follow the belief that we are most likely to be under attack from Satan when we are trying to do a good work for the Lord. However, there was another conclusion I came to from watching the squirrel. God never intended for squirrels to walk across power lines, so one of the biggest reasons for the squirrel's torment that day is that he was somewhere that he never should have been. How many times have you or I had to ask God or our parents for help when the problem could have been avoided if we had just stayed away from the wrong crowd or asked for God's direction before we made the wrong decision?

Where They Should Not Have Stayed

This leads me to another point I want to bring out: when we are in the wrong place, we tend to get comfortable. I have been thinking a lot the past few weeks about the Hebrews' time in Egypt. I am sure most of us are quick to feel sorry for the persecution they suffered and feel they really did need deliverance. But what I have been thinking about lately is what happened during those silent years? Most people believe that it was the plan of God for the Israelites to stay in Egypt and grow into a great nation, and most would agree that the story of the Exodus was a great showcase of the power of God. The question I raise is "Was such deliverance necessary?" Joseph did prophesy that God would come and bring them back to the land of Canaan, but I wonder did God try sooner rather than later and they refused to go? No one knows the plan of God, but for the purpose of illustration, let's imagine that the Israelites did, on their own, overstay their welcome in Egypt as the Bible tells us, but let's also imagine that God was moving in the hearts of the people to return to Canaan, and they refused to heed his call. We know that it was the plan of God for them to be in Egypt for a time, to weather the storm of the famine, but we also know it was God's plan for them to dwell in Canaan. In

... when we are in the wrong place, we tend to get comfortable.

my outside-the-box thinking, I just cannot help but believe that God never intended the sojourn in Egypt to last 400 years. And I feel that the persecution from the pharaoh who knew not Joseph was the instrument to put them on their way back to Canaan. Yes, I think God was ready for the Exodus long before the children of Israel, but they were comfortable in the land of Egypt, maybe like some of us living in the land of sin. Maybe we could even include Lot living in Sodom. Lot and his family were so comfortable that they did not even know they were in the need of deliverance.

I do not want you to think that I am a Biblical scholar, but for my purpose, let's assume that God only intended for the Israelites to stay in Egypt for a few years. I'm sure that early on they would talk about the day they would return to their homeland.

Probably during the life of Joseph, things were good, so they never planned for their return. Then as time passed on and as the original family members died, I bet few ever even mentioned going back to Canaan. If someone did bring the subject up, the scoffers more than likely said, "Life is great in Egypt; let us stay here."

Oh, it's so easy to pick apart the lives of the Israelites, but what about you and me? If you were asked the question today, could you answer, "Yes, I am right where God wants me to be"? Or would your answer be "I don't have a clue"? The problem you have that you are in need of deliverance from today may not be an attack from Satan; it may just be God telling you it is time to move on. It may or may not be because of sin in your life. Maybe something good you are doing was the right thing then but not now; maybe it's time to let some things go and move on to something greater. Those answers I don't know, but my point is that we need to pray and examine all areas of our lives, so we know how to pray correctly, rather than to just blame it all on the devil.

God will show us the way and help us to avoid Satan if we just ask.

Isn't it amazing what you can learn from animals?

It is even more amazing what you can do if you seek God in prayer and ask his direction first. There are many of us who find ourselves facing difficult decisions now with seemingly no right answer and, in many cases, just because of some of our past incorrect decisions. But we just need to stay "steadfast in the faith," as Peter was telling us above and trust God to lead us in the right direction and vow to Him to follow his leading. God will show us the way and help us to avoid Satan if we just ask. Turn to him today with all your cares. Climb down off that wire; you've been in Egypt long enough.

Always Ask God

In the course of my normal Bible reading this week, I was reading in the book of Joshua. It is a good book with many encouraging stories of how God led his people to conquer the land of Canaan. One story in particular caught my attention, and I will share my thoughts with you. In Joshua 9, we read of an encounter with some ambassadors from Gibeon. These people had heard stories of how God had blessed the children of Israel and how they were winning battle after battle and everyone was falling at their feet. So, the inhabitants of Gibeon came up with a plan—they were going to make a peace treaty with the invaders.

Let me remind you that God had instructed Joshua and all the leaders of Israel that during the conquest of Canaan there was to be total destruction of the inhabitants, no survivors. In modern war terms, that would be a "scorched earth policy." However, it seems that the Gibeonites knew that God had told

Joshua to use the scorched earth approach and not to make peace with any of the inhabitants of Canaan, so they devised a plan. They put on old clothes and old shoes and packed their donkeys with old wine and moldy bread to make it appear that they had made

... there is nothing too big for God, and more importantly, there is nothing too small for God.

a long journey, not that they just lived around the corner, so to speak. They were smart; they smoothly acted this out, and they were able to catch Joshua and his close advisors by surprise, and they quickly made a deal with them. "How?" you ask? And "Why?" you ask? Well, it seems that Joshua made the mistake that we all make from time to time; I suppose he thought this was a small matter and no need to bother God with it. Rabbit trail alert! Two things you should always remember: there is nothing too big for God, and more importantly, there is nothing too small for God. One of my newer expressions is "We are all just kids playing in God's sandbox." Let me unpack that for you, at the risk of a rabbit trail from a rabbit trail. Do not compare yourself to men; compare yourself to God. If you compare yourself to men, you might end up with a self-esteem problem, but if you compare yourself and everyone else to God, you see that we are all pretty much the same. Relative to God, there is not much difference between the bank president and the homeless man. Getting back to my point, when you compare your prayer needs to God's ability, there is not much difference between what you consider big and small.

So, on the surface, it looked like a simple decision. These people seemed to have traveled a great distance, and they were not going to be a problem. Therefore, Joshua made a big mistake just trying to help God out a little bit and not worrying Him about this small decision. Well, in the end, Joshua found out the truth, but because they had made an oath before God, Joshua adjured the people to keep this peace treaty, but the Gibeonites were to be slaves.

... when you compare your prayer needs to God's ability, there is not much difference between what you consider big and small.

I guess I've said all that just to say this: how many times do we get ourselves into a mess and then ask God for help to fix it, when we wouldn't have been in the mess if we had just asked for His direction to begin with? As years go by, I hear myself sounding more and more like my parents, as I'm sure others of you who are also parents find yourselves in the same boat. But we start to see how God feels toward us when we say to our children, "Why didn't you just ask me first?" Fill in the blanks on what the problem is, but it is hard to fix problems after someone else has "worked on them" and made them worse. So, the next time you, or especially I, have a decision to make: ASK GOD. In the end, you will save Him time and trouble if you ask His direction first rather than asking His help in the end.

We Are Healed

Have you ever waited for someone and thought he or she might be late and just did not understand why because they were usually on time. Then all of the sudden, you look across the parking lot (or crowd in the store or ten other scenarios) and see that after a couple of cars moved, they were there all the time. Both of you looking for each other but just could not make connection.

I feel that many reading this book may be waiting on God to move or to make His appearance on the scene. Or maybe you don't have a relationship with God, and you just have an empty feeling, a longing for something more. Nevertheless, as with the example I started with, someone waiting for God to move in his or her life but not realizing that He has already done what is necessary, is kind of like my parking lot example.

This Scripture has been on my mind for several days in the context that I have just described. Isaiah

53:5 says, *"But He was wounded for our transgressions, He was bruised for our iniquities; the chastisement for our peace was upon Him, And by His stripes we are healed".*

I want you to think about a couple of things with me, but first I want to make sure you are aware that in this verse, Isaiah is prophesying about Christ's death on the cross. So, if you believe and agree with me on that, when we look at the middle of the verse, notice it says "for our peace," that tells me that peace is available for you and me. We don't have to wait for God to do anything else. And in the last part of the verse, it says "by His stripes we are healed." It doesn't say, "If we try to be good, we might be healed;" it says we are healed. God, through His son Jesus Christ, has done all He needs to do. The rest is up to you. No, I don't understand why everyone isn't healed or delivered the first time they pray. Someday, God will answer those questions for us. But for today, I know that Jesus gave His all on the cross. So, I guess the next move is up to you.

Have You Done All You Can, or Are You Serious With Your Prayers?

Some years ago, I read an article about the McGruders, and in the paragraph that caught my attention, Carroll was telling of a time during which Priscilla was struggling with cancer when he saw her standing on a Bible. When he inquired why, she said that, paraphrasing some of Paul's words to the Ephesians, she had done all she could and she was standing on the Word. I am sure we have all felt that way at some point, whether it was due to sickness, loss of a loved one, loss of a job, financial difficulties, or the list could go on. I don't doubt Priscilla's faith or her efforts, but for the rest of us, have we done all we can?

It just happened that the next day, Dr. Tony Evans on his program, *The Urban Alternative,* was preaching on fasting. Moreover, he just happened to mention that if you think you have tried everything, he asks, "Have you fasted?" As Jesus said in Matthew 17:21, *"However, this kind does not go out except by prayer and fasting"* when he was talking about the disciples' inability to cast out a demon. While your problem may not involve demonic possession, I believe the principle is the same. Moreover, I see Dr. Evans' point that if you have not tried fasting, then maybe you have not done all you can.

While prayer can be a time of petition, it is also a time of reflection and a time for you to listen for that still small voice of God.

So, have we done all we can? Some may but most of us probably have not, so let us look at a few suggestions to make our prayers more effective. James 5:16 says, *"Confess faults to one another, and pray for one another, that you may be healed. The effectual fervent prayer of a righteous man availeth much."* Let us discover some ways to make your prayers both fervent and effectual. To begin to see your prayers answered, first you must develop a consistent prayer life. Prayer is not just a time to give God your "shopping list," so to speak. While prayer can be a time of petition, it is also a time of reflection and a time for you to listen for that still small voice of God. Being able to commune with God on a daily basis is a first step to see real change in your life.

As the title suggests, if we want to see God move in a life-changing way, we must get serious with our prayers. As I say from time to time, don't think I've mastered all the secrets of prayer or of living a Christian life, but this is another time when I want to share my studies and my own struggles. In James 4:2, the last part of the verse says, *"You have not because you ask not,"* so to ask correctly, your prayers have to get past "God bless me." First steps may be actually sitting down and writing down what you want God to do in your life. Are you familiar with smart goals? Smart goals have been a buzzword in the personal and business development game for some time, and they are comprised of words from each of the letters in the word "smart." Now there are many variations, but for my purpose, I have chosen these: Specific, Measurable, Agreed Upon, Relevant, Timely. Most

... if we want to see God move in a life-changing way, we must get serious with our prayers.

would never consider prayer from a business perspective, but maybe that is because most do not actually "get down to business" with God.

It is strange that I am suggesting writing things down because I am the world's worst at making lists of any kind. But in this case, whether you actually put it on paper or not, it is crucial that you have a list of your prayer concerns if you really want to see action. I discourage anyone from having vague prayers, such as praying for the lost. While that might be relevant, it is surely not specific or measurable. If would be much better to call someone by name or at least say everyone on my street. How can you tell if your prayers are being answered if they are not measureable? There are several words to fit in the "A" slot, but I like "Agreed Upon;" that means you and God have agreed upon something and have committed to seeing it through. These smart goal attributes are a great way to seeing your prayers answered.

I do not want anyone to feel that I am "Super Christian," but I just want to share the things that God has done in my life and hope that it can be a help and a blessing to others. In relation to these smart goal prayers, a few months ago I prayed that I would meet a specific person at a neutral location to have a casual conversation about a specific subject. In less than a week, that conversation occurred. Because of the specific nature of that prayer, I can say without a doubt it was answered. But to tell the rest of the story, what was discussed during that conversation didn't come to fruition. Using that example, God answers all earnest prayers, but He does not give them all a rubber stamp of YES. Some are yes, but some are no, and in that case, the yes to one prayer makes it easier to accept the no in the other.

Once you begin using these smart goals in your prayers, you can use your prayer journal as a check-list to measure your progress. In some situations, you may be left without a clear direction for your prayers. If you have cancer or some other serious illness, your prayers will naturally be more direct and to the point. But for some other needs, you may need to pray to determine what your prayer should be in that event.

... we serve a big God and He is able to do exceedingly above all we ask and think.

That is where you can use the "Agreed Upon" portion of the goals.

A very important part of getting serious with your prayers is getting to the root of the problem. Some people think money will solve all their problems, but I once heard a wise man say, "If money can fix it, it's not a problem." Money, or the lack thereof, is usually a symptom of deeper issues, and those are the things that you really need to talk to God about. Did I say it would be easy? Or that I could give you all the answers in 500 words or less? I do believe that God answers prayer, but for you to better see His answers, I am suggesting to you that your prayers be "measurable" so that in the end you can share with others how God unquestionably answered your prayer. I do not know what the problem is that you are facing, but I do know we serve a big God and He is able to do exceedingly above all we ask and think. And I don't know what you've tried and how hard you've prayed. I'm just suggesting that before you give up and think that you have done all you can and God hasn't answered, examine your heart and ask yourself have you truly done all you can. Even then, when you have done all you can, just stand and keep you faith in God, and remember, as I have ended so many columns and radio programs, believe the full Gospel and live a full life.

God's Economy

I really do not have much to say about the state of U.S. politics or the economy. We have gone through a very divisive political season, and hopefully, now we will see some change and some healing. The fact is if you put your trust in one man or one woman to change things, you will be extremely dissatisfied. For only God can change America, and it will have to start with His people turning back to Him.

I do want to talk a little bit about the economy, God's economy. While it has taken some time, I am to a point where I trust God and His provision for my family and myself. To begin, we have to get to the point where doing God's will is our priority and at times just let the chips fall where they may. No, I am not talking about preachers. I am talking about everyone. We get too hung up on saying that ministry is just what goes on behind the pulpit. God has called all – yes, *all* – of His people to be ministers.

Something I have learned about God's economy is that while you might devote much of your time to ministry work, you might never be paid in the way we all expect. However, it is not always about what you make but what you have to spend. In this world in which we live, so many are judged by what they do, by their occupation. You ask people what they are, and they say "doctor," "lawyer," "dogcatcher," or whatever. I learned a long time ago that what we do should not define us.

... to truly be involved in ministry, it has to be a lifestyle, and you have to trust that God will provide.

I am new to Facebook, and I have been trying to add and update some of the information. One of the questions it asked was "Who you are?" or "What do you do?" It was one of those. I do not recall the exact wording. I put "gospel singer." Do I draw a paycheck from that? No. But that is who I am or at least what I consider myself to be, and that is one of my contributions to the work of God. Yes, we do earn something from singing sometimes, but it is usually passed on to another charity or something. It is not about the money. The point is, to truly be involved in ministry, it has to be a lifestyle, and you have to trust that God will provide. So, I have invested probably over $3,000 in music equipment in the past couple of years. I am scared to really figure it up, and I think that Ricky has less than $100 stuck in a coffee can that we have received from offerings and donations, and we will most likely give it away. Is that a good investment? Maybe not, but it is a God investment. That is why we have to trust in God's economy. Whether personally or with a group, I always seem to have a place to sing, and our financial situation is better than it was a year ago. Many times, you will see that in God's economy, it is not about what you take in, but you might see a supernatural reduction in costs. Either way, it pays to trust in Him.

The first part of this chapter was edited from one of my Facebook posts from the fall of 2016, but I have a little more to say on the topic. I have mentioned directly or alluded to some of the principles discussed in this chapter in other parts of the book.

... if we are to rely on God's promises and His protection, we must be His. We must be saved.

At the risk of belaboring the point, I just cannot stress enough the importance of living in God's economy. As I mentioned in the chapter entitled "Find the Lord Before You Need Him," if we are to rely on

God's promises and His protection, we must be His. We must be saved.

First of all, we must put God first in our lives and in all of our thinking. Proverbs 3:5-6 says, *"Trust in the Lord with all thine heart; and lean not unto thine own understanding. In all thy ways acknowledge him, and he shall direct thy paths."* Just a small rabbit trail, but so many times when we study the Bible, it seems too hard to understand, but this portion is very sim-

To truly put God first, we must worship Him.

ple. "All means all," as a pastor friend of mine likes to say, so it is very simple to read and understand. The big "but" comes along when we try to live it. While reading that verse, another good saying comes to mind: "good preaching but hard living."

To truly put God first, we must worship Him. Let us break this down a bit. Worship Him with our time, our talents, and our finances. A few of you just said that I have quit preaching and started meddling and then closed the book, but for the rest of you, let us continue. There are so many references and examples in the Bible about worship I don't think I need to go into any detail for the purposes of this book. I think, however, we will all agree that corporate worship in a Bible-believing church is a must for every

Christian. Once we are members of a local church, that gives us many opportunities to use our talents for the advancement of God's kingdom, but we must not stop there because we will find still other opportunities to be of service to God. We just need to keep our eyes and mind open.

As I have said before, this isn't all about me, and I don't claim to be "Super Christian," but I just tend to use myself for an example and tell not only the good but also sometimes the bad and the ugly. This example might be part of the ugly. I have been involved in what most would call ministry for over twenty years. I have sung, preached, taught, written, and been on the radio. I am not bragging or complaining, just stating the facts for those who may not know. I do not know if this is really bad or just human nature, but I have always wanted more. I always wanted something better—maybe to be paid or better paid, maybe to have a full-time, paying ministry position—but it has never happened. Who knows, it may never happen. As I sit here working on this book, I have no real intention of it being a best seller. As a matter of fact, I will most likely try to have it published as cheaply as possible, so I can give many of them away to those in need. But let me tell you what has happened. My thinking has changed. Prayer changes things, and God has changed my thinking. It has taken a while, but now I see that ministry is not about status, money, or recognition but about simply doing what God asks you to do and letting Him worry about the rest.

In my case that has been accepting the fact that I am to take advantage of the ministry opportunities that I am presented with and then carry on with my secular job to bring in a paycheck and then let God work out all the details and make ends meet. We would all like to sing or minister at the biggest church in every town, but often that is not where the need is and that is not where God would have us to go. So, when I say worship God with our talents, I don't mean that we get to pick the jobs. We must be willing to go where we are needed. Most of you

Whatever great or small you can do, do it for the glory of God.

would not be in a hurry to go sing at the nursing home or the homeless shelter, but I can speak from experience that it is in those situations that you receive the greatest blessings. For the record, I had to stop typing to wipe the tears because those in need enjoy your singing the best, and I count it all joy to see someone come down to the altar while I am singing, and if that's the case, I can sing all day. Whatever great or small you can do, do it for the glory of God. It may be just taking out the trash in the fellowship hall, it may be working in the nursery, but it is all important, and we must all be willing.

How could one write about God's economy and not mention giving? By putting God first, we accept and realize that everything is the Lord's and that we are just managers. Our time, our talents, our money—it is all His; He just allows us to manage it. In the last couple of paragraphs, I discussed the use of time and talents, and I am sure someone reading this is thinking, "Yes, I would do more for God if I did not have to work so much." Well, maybe you do not have to work so much; you just need to trust God more. Yes, I understand. I think I mentioned in an earlier chapter that I am a recovering workaholic. While I am not totally there yet, I can say the recovery process gets easier as you get older. Learning to trust in God and not in the work of your own hands is a big part of living in God's economy. As I said above, it is not about how much you make but how you can get by on less. God will help meet those needs if you devote more time to His work.

I do not have a magic formula. I cannot tell you how much to do and how much to give. All I can do is to let you know that God's economy works. In my opinion, the most important thing is consistency. In other words, you should practice regular church attendance, participation, and giving. Then God will expect you to grow. If you can only attend church once a week, then attend once a week, but make it every week and strive to attend more as time goes on. The rule of tithing is ten percent; most of us are familiar with that number. My suggestion is do not wait to start giving until you can give ten percent. If you need to start with ten dollars, start with ten dollars. Then increase to twenty and maybe then to fifty, but whatever the amount, give regularly and consistently. Lastly do whatever you can in the service of God. It can be within the walls of the church, but it does not have to be limited to those four walls. Use your talents for God whatever they may be. There are no guarantees that you will be rich and famous, but you will be blessed.

God Has a Plan

Several years ago while covering a news story I heard a speaker, who happened to be a pastor, addressing the gathering on the topic of not letting your past determine your future. The event was an open campus graduation for students who had dropped out of school but who now had gone back and obtained the right to be high school graduates. While he did not identify the name of his example, at first he talked about the problems that Abraham Lincoln had experienced in his life. I won't take the time to go into them all, but Lincoln's life was filled with hardship and disappointments, and in the end, he was in the place God meant for him to be and at God's timing.

The more I thought on the subject, my mind went to the book of Genesis and the story of Joseph. While it is too long to cover here, his was also a story of hardship and of disappointment in the beginning. However, in the end, God revealed his purpose, and in Genesis 45:5, Joseph reveals the truth to his brothers: *"Now therefore be not grieved, nor angry with yourselves, that ye sold me hither: for God did send me before you to preserve life."* In both cases, the rest is history, as people say. In the end, both men led their country through difficult times.

The thought that kept going through my mind as I heard the pastor talk about Lincoln was that God knew a long time before 1861 that America would be caught in the midst of a civil war. Just like he had spoken to Abraham that his descendants would spend time in a foreign land long before the birth of Joseph. In both cases, God had a plan for these great men, but I believe it was the circumstances they faced in life that gave them the strength and character to fulfill God's purposes for them.

Now some ten years after I first composed this, so much has changed in my life and in America. The point for today is that God knew then what I would face, and He knew the challenges this country would experience, but He also has a plan. I don't know anything about your life or the challenges you face, but maybe, just maybe, they are part of God's plan for you. God uses the hard things in life to build and define our character, to mold us like clay on the potter's wheel, and to make us more into his image. Allow God to have his way in your life and let him help you to grow and be the person He wants you to be.

Don't Be a Settler

Some time back, I saw a couple of commercials with the actors dressed in nineteenth century-Western attire. I am not sure of the company that produced them—I think a large media outlet—but the message was that they were settlers because they settled for less than the best that was available. As one who has always loved Westerns, this was quick to catch my attention because it was such a great play on words to equate those who settled the Old West with people who settle for just anything because in reality they are the opposite. The pioneers of the American West were anything but settlers by this definition, far

from it. They made a way where there was no way, and many gave their lives in the process. No, they were not settlers.

While I know none of you are pioneers traveling the American West in Conestoga wagons, are you a settler? In your daily life, do you settle for less than the very best? Do not take me the wrong way, for I know that many of us cannot afford the best of everything that the retail world has to offer, but that is not what I am getting at. In a spiritual sense, do you settle for less than the best that God has for you? In fact, I think for many of us the answer is yes. So, why is that answer yes, and what are we going to do about it?

Why are we settlers? In reality, the why does not matter. Yes, some root-cause analysis might help us get to the bottom of things and change our path, but in this case, we must turn things over to God and let Him change our attitudes and our actions. In many cases, first we have to realize that God wants to bless us and enable us to do His work and to live abundant lives. Nowhere in the Bible does it say that the blessings and gifts were only for Peter, Paul, and Mary or for Mark, Luke, and John. We need to get ahold of the fact that those gifts and blessing are for us, too. Paul says in 1 Corinthians 12:7, *"But the manifestation of the Spirit is given to every man to profit withal."* And in another version, it says "for the common good." In this case, we know Paul is talking about Christians but not just men, women also, so to break it down, all Christians are given a measure of faith and spirit, and it is up to us to use them.

So, then you say, maybe you have some faith and spirit, but it isn't as powerful as that of the disciples. To that, Paul also says in Romans 8:11 that the same spirit that rose Christ from the dead dwells in you. So, is that spirit powerful enough to accomplish the

Do you know God's will and purpose for your life?

tasks set before you? I think that it is. It comes down to a couple of questions. Do you know God's will and purpose for your life? And do you believe He has the power to accomplish this through you? As a Christian, you have the power within you; it is up to you to exercise your faith to see it accomplish great things for God.

Upon more thought and discussion, it becomes clear that there are at least two degrees of settlers. First, those who are just getting by, and second, those who look like they are setting the world on fire for Christ but maybe still not doing all they could. Thirdly, there in a significant group that is somewhere in between. This chapter is written for those in the first group, and most of you may not even realize you are settling because you have not taken the time to seek God and allow Him to reveal His plan and purpose for your life.

He has a plan for us all, and He wants us to be both the workers in the field spreading His good news and those sharing in the blessings of His love and grace.

One thing I would like you all to realize: I do, without a doubt, believe that God has control over everything. While I do not understand it, He is concerned with each of us, and He will guide us if we will listen. Sometimes, that means we have to wait on Him to show us the right thing to do at the right time. The point I am getting at in this rabbit trail is that I have been stuck on this chapter for a couple of weeks now. A couple of weeks ago, I taught a Sunday school lesson on this topic, hoping to clear my ideas to complete this chapter. Well, that didn't seem to work. So, being a patient fellow with many other irons in the fire, I tended to the ones that seemed hotter. Yesterday in Sunday school, our classroom was warm, and my wife, knowing she would find some paper in my Bible, just grabbed the first thing that it opened up to and began to fan herself. Yes, I have a point, and I'll get there in a minute. After several minutes, she handed me back the paper for me to place back in my Bible. Before doing so, I began to read it. I don't recall why it was even there as it had been written about ten years before. As I read it, strangely enough, it fit in with the lesson our teacher was sharing, so when there was a break, I read it to the class. Not only did it fit yesterday's lesson but also it fits with the message of this chapter. So, with slight editing, the following passage is from that column:

Throughout the course of life, whoever you are, there are points that some will call "defining moments." Times when it seems your whole life hangs in the balance. Situations where you must make decisions that could change the direction of your life. Today we are going back to a time when the children of Israel were facing just such a moment. Let us learn from them and apply what we learn to our own lives.

In Deuteronomy 30, Moses is addressing his people for the last time. You could say he is preaching his last sermon. He brings things to a point in verse 19 when he says, *"I call Heaven and earth to record today against you. I have set before you life and death, blessing and cursing. Therefore, choose life, so that both you and your seed may live."* Yes, I am pro-life, but the phrase "choose life" has an even greater meaning to me, and I hope you will see as you read on.

In the book of John 10:10, Jesus says, *"The thief does not come except to steal and to kill and to destroy. I have come so that they might have life, and that they might have it more abundantly."* Many Christian have heard that so much that it has almost become a cliché. Keep those two verses of scripture in mind, and let me tell you a little background of the name for my newspaper and online column "Live a Full Life." Over twenty years ago, I began a weekly radio program on a local AM radio station. One of the first things you need to do before undertaking such a feat is to come up with a name. Moreover, more importantly, it has to be an appropriate name and one that symbolizes what you believe. When someone mentions the term "full gospel," most associate that with a belief in all of the operation of the gifts of the Spirit and, as some would say, the "Pentecostal" experience.

The point I would like to make to you today is that salvation is not just for when you die. Once a person trusts Jesus as their Savior, yes, you have the hope of Heaven to be your eternal home, but you do not have to wait until you die to receive the benefits of that choice. When Jesus said He came that you might have life more abundantly, He did not mean after the resurrection, He meant now.

If you are a Christian and you feel you are not living that abundant life, don't let Satan cheat you out of anything. The promise of an abundant life is a free gift and available to all that trust in Christ. I will not tell you that everything will always be roses, but God will provide the grace you need to see you through. God always has enough, and He is always on time, even when we do not think so. Trust Him with your life today. In answer to Moses' question at the beginning, choose life. And, remember, believe the full gospel and live a full live.

That column illustrates my point that if you are not living the abundant life God has for you, you are settling. I do not want anyone to be continually discontented, but do not settle for anything less than the best that God has for you. Believe all of the promises in the Bible and trust your heart and life to Jesus, and you can live that full and abundant life.

Change Equals Growth

We now have children living in four different states, with the farthest being around 1,700 miles apart. As most of you would agree, this is not the ideal situation, and while we do not often dwell on it, my wife and I are not very happy about it. Patience lets us understand that there is some good in almost everything. This morning while looking through a magazine, I noticed an advertisement for a little-known fast food restaurant. While there is none within 500 miles of our home, I can say that in the past year, because of my scattered children, I have eaten at one of their locations. As I began to reminisce, I thought of other places that I have been to and seen that, without traveling to see some of the kids, we would have never visited. We were just in Maryland, only for a few miles, but my first time ever. We saw the Alamo and Sea World, both on Christmas Eve, while visiting my daughter and her husband, whom I am proud to say, is serving in the US Army, and their two (now three) children. Just last week, I had the pleasure of dining with an old friend whom I had not seen face to face in over twenty years because, you guessed it, we traveled through his city on the way home from visiting family.

Later on in that same magazine, I briefly looked at a story of a woman who developed a new variety of make-up because of a skin condition she endured. While that did not bring anything specifically to mind, we are all aware of products invented, refined, or developed because of a need. Maybe because of a new situation or because someone said, "I cannot take it anymore; something has to change." Nevertheless, as the saying goes, necessity is the mother of invention. The point I am moving towards is change is necessary and positive change is beneficial. Thanks to computers, typists no longer need whiteout. I have used Google twice in the last hundred words or so, and now half of you are wondering what for. Yes, change can be a good thing.

But what if change is unwelcome? Or even forced upon us? James tells us to count it all joy when we are in diverse trials. He goes on to say that the trying of our faith produces patience. So, it appears it is all up to us on how we react to change. While it may not be in our power to stop it or to avoid it, it is in our power how we deal with it, and we can make it either positive or negative. When the next change comes to your life, with God's help, make it a positive.

Whatever Your Circumstances, You Can Be a Blessing

Many times, we let our circumstances overwhelm us to the point where we seem useless in our own eyes. We get to feeling like we cannot even help ourselves, so why even try to make a difference for the kingdom of God? Maybe it is because of age or health issues, but it can easily be just because of poor self-esteem. Many of us sell ourselves short every day by belittling our influence to those we regularly come into contact with. As the old saying goes, "You

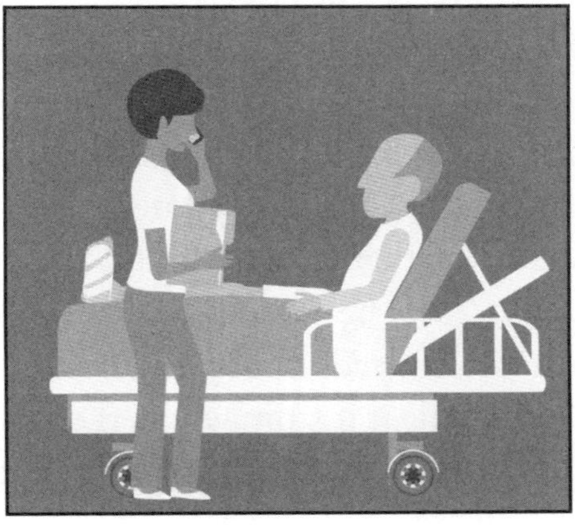

might be the only Bible that some people ever read." And read our lives as Christians, they do. You might be able to fool some of the people you casually meet each Sunday at church, but you can't fool the skeptics—they do not just listen to your words. They also watch your actions.

I began thinking on this subject after seeing someone whom had previously been helpful to my father in dealing with his illness in his final months. Many of dad's caregivers have, since his passing, commented to me on how he blessed them, on how easy it was to help and care for him. The most memorable to me was the words of a volunteer firefighter. One day we were talking, and I told him thanks and

Your words and your spirit can determine whether you are a blessing or a curse in their eyes.

how much I appreciated the times that he, and others from his station, had helped dad get back on his feet after he had fallen. The man said that he did not mind at all. In fact, he said that he enjoyed helping dad because he enjoyed talking with him.

When you look at it from where the rubber meets the road, dad's greatest Christian influence may not have been when he was standing as a pastor behind a pulpit but by his gentle spirit while he was on his sick

> *Sow words of blessing, and the Lord will return to you a harvest of benefits.*

bed. This is just one example in a million. You may be reading this from a hospital bed today, thinking that you cannot do anything for anyone. Your life and the way you respond to your situation can speak volumes to your caregivers. Your words and your spirit can determine whether you are a blessing or a curse in their eyes. Sow words of blessing, and the Lord will return to you a harvest of benefits. I have been told countless stories from nursing home workers of how they are blessed by their patients, so never sell yourself short.

The point of this chapter applies to all of us: at some point, we can be a blessing to someone. It starts when we lose sight of our failings and cast our eyes on God and His power to transform us and to bless our efforts. Sometimes, God will use us in spite of ourselves. Yes, when we try so hard and fall flat on our face, so to speak, and we think all is lost, God will find a way to use that situation to help that person we were trying to reach or maybe even someone else. Yes, we can all be a blessing to someone.

It is important to realize that we are all different.

In reality, it took me over forty years to make practical application of that truth in my life. In the years since, I have been better able to serve and deal with others because I have learned that everyone doesn't see things as I do, many things not even close. As it relates to ministry in the kingdom of God, you can reach people that I might never even be able to talk to. You might have just the words someone needs to hear. You will come in contact with people I may never see.

Never look down on yourself for any reason, except maybe for comfortably living in sin and enjoying it, because if you have accepted Jesus as Savior, you are God's child, and you have value and potential. In Jesus' name, be a blessing to someone today.

Have It Your Way

While traveling through these United States of America the other day, I saw a sign that made a good point. If you have ever read any of my writings, you have noticed by now that I am always on the lookout for something to catch my eye to write about. Well, this one did. On the exit door of a popular nationwide fast food chain, which prides itself on doing things the way the customer wants it, the sign reads "PUSH." But then in smaller letters under that, it said, "you can have it your way and pull, but this door is pretty stubborn."

The first thought that came to my mind was that all of us have that deep inward desire to do things our own way, and unfortunately, sometimes we choose that way rather than God's way. In our desire to help God out and do things our way, it is important to realize that when we make a wrong choice and do not see immediate judgment, it does not mean that God approves of our choice. If you remember, Satan told Eve in the garden, "you will not surely die." While she did not die an immediate physical death, she did die a spiritual death and became separated from the presence of God and was forced to leave the paradise of the Garden of Eden, as well as other consequences.

As Christians, we must give up on the world's "have it your way" mentality and turn our lives and our efforts to God.

In Numbers 20, Moses is angry at the children of Israel and strikes the rock twice, rather than speaking to it as God had commanded, and it cost him a trip to the Promised Land. If you will read in verse 10, it appears that Moses takes the credit for the water coming from the rock. Even then, God's judgment was not immediate and public, but Moses and Aaron were not allowed to enter into the Promised Land because of their actions of doubting God's ability to provide for His people and also in part for acting in haste and in anger.

Paul says at least twice in the New Testament, once in 1 Corinthians 6:12: *"All things are lawful unto me, but all things are not expedient: all things are law-*

ful for me, but I will not be brought under the power of any." As Christians, we must give up on the world's "have it your way" mentality and turn our lives and our efforts to God. Just because we do not see immediate judgment does not mean we are on the right path, especially if we feel that still small voice of God telling us to go a different way.

Many times as it relates to ministry, we use clichés like "God opened the door" or, at times, "God closed the door" to describe His directing power. But in other areas of life, we seem to ignore His direction. While it may be a new concept to some of you, I feel we need to seek God's direction in all areas of our lives, much the same as in which some would consider ministry. Because, my friend, it is all about ministry; it is all about seeing the lost saved and the saved encouraged. When we begin to live with that mindset, we will be much closer to Jesus' plans for the church in His Great Commission.

... we need to seek God's direction in all areas of our lives ...

God gave us a free will and the ability to choose the path we will take, and if we are strong enough or if we use a crowbar, we can "pull" that door and get it open, but that is not the way it is intended to work.

God has a plan for each and every one of us, and He will give us hints and direction to show us the way. I believe He puts certain obstacles in our path to make us stop and think about what we are doing; this is an example of a closed door. Do we really want it our way? Open your heart to God today and listen to his direction. Undoubtedly, you will find He has a better plan. Let us forget about our way and try God's way.

Visions of Heaven

The Apostle Paul tells us of a heavenly experience in 2 Corinthians 12. In verse 2, he says, *"I know a man in Christ fourteen years before (whether in the body, I do not know; or outside of the body, I do not know; God knows) such a one was caught up to the third Heaven."*

I believe Paul is speaking of the time in Acts 14 when he was stoned near the city of Iconium and assumed dead. His friends and fellow believers then prayed for him, and he recovered. One of the reasons I believe this is the fact that Paul mentions this stoning just a few verses before in 2 Corinthians 11: 25, *"Three times I was beaten with rods, once I was stoned, three times I was shipwrecked. I have spent a night and a day in the deep."*

But let's not debate that issue, the point is Paul goes on to say in verse 4 *"that he was caught up into Paradise and heard unspeakable words, which it is not allowed for a man to utter."* I believe that Paul got a glimpse of heaven, maybe just what he needed to help him keep going on his journey. More importantly, I believe this is just a little more evidence that heaven is real. While I've not seen heaven myself, I believe that it is real. I have faith.

Many stories have been told about people who have had what are termed "near death experiences." And I'm sure some of you believe and some of you don't. I choose to tell you this story today: it may not be as special to you as it is to me because it is of an experience my father had a short time before his death in 2007. Dad had been in the hospital for several days with pneumonia and with a broken ankle. Later, we learned that fluid had also built up around his heart, which probably was affecting his condition on this day.

While I've not seen heaven myself, I believe that it is real. I have faith.

But on this particular day while I was by his bedside, with an RN on the other side, his whole countenance changed. His face had a look of shock and awe. The nurse, sensing something was wrong, asked if he was okay. He didn't speak for a minute but then said he was fine. Nothing more was said until later that

Max Hansen

night when he told me that, at that earlier point, he thought he was dying and that he did see the lights of Heaven. He has since commented that a few minutes after this experience, he grabbed the pen and paper he kept by his bed because he wanted to write down what he saw. But he said that as he stared at the paper, the words just wouldn't come because words could not describe what he had seen.

Heaven is real, sports fans, not just because my dad says but because of my faith in my Heavenly Father. Are you ready? You may not believe the Apostle Paul, you may or may not believe Max Hansen, but I believe, and I'm ready.

Clean Out the Clutter

The other evening my wife Veronica, was doing a massive cleaning in our kitchen. Besides floors, walls, and curtains, she began the task of taking down and washing the decorative items atop our cabinets. In the midst of this, she asked me to run an errand, and while I was gone, the Holy Spirit spoke to me the inspiration for this chapter. I walked back in the house upon my return and wrote out a whole page of notes. I think these points apply to us all in the natural and in the spiritual.

First of all, clean out the clutter from your heart, soul, and spirit to allow God to speak to and work through you. I am focusing on things in a spiritual sense, but in some cases, you need to clean out the material clutter if it is hampering your relationship with God. Ephesians 4:31 tells us, "Let all bitterness, and wrath, and anger, and clamour, and evil speaking, be put away from you, with all malice." In other words, don't do it. Likewise James 1:21 from the Amplified Bible, Classic Edition (AMPC) says, *"So get rid of all uncleanness and the rampant outgrowth of wickedness, and in a humble (gentle, modest) spirit receive and welcome the Word which implanted and rooted [in your hearts] contains the power to save your souls."* Note the correlation in this verse linking removing sin with receiving the Word and the power of salvation.

Let us not worry about whether the glass is half-full or half empty, but let us focus on the fact that the glass can only hold so much. While we do not truly know and understand the capabilities of our brain, experientially we know how much we can handle. Therefore, if our brain becomes overloaded, we cannot take any more in. God, being the gentleman He is, will not come in and clean house for us, so we must remove some of the "stuff" so that there will be more room for His Spirit.

Not only does clutter take up space, but it takes up or time. Not saying it is all clutter or has no value, but back to my earlier example, Veronica's knick-knacks need to be taken down occasionally and cleaned if they are to continue to look nice and maintain some value. By the same token, our spiritual clutter robs us of time and mental energy. How many times have you thought about something, worried about something, and saw no change. Just the same merry go round over and over. As my friend Philip says, "Worry is like a rocking chair—it keeps you busy, but you go nowhere."

What do I mean by spiritual clutter, you ask? Here

are some examples of the things I am talking about: hurtful memories of conversations with a friend or relative that did not go like you wished. You could be replaying the same bad scenario in your mind again and again, but it always ends the same. Self-pity is a killer, and it makes negative references to yourself, your friends, or family members. One of the biggest hang-ups for most of us is continuing to focus on past sins, failures, and mistakes; these prevent us from moving forward in God's grace and love. And don't forget about the "if onlys." Oh, how we think life would be great if only we had a better job or a hundred other things to fill-in-the-blank. My list could go on and on, but I think you will see what I mean by clutter.

... our spiritual clutter robs us of time and mental energy.

So many times I have wondered, "Should I do this?" or "Should I have done that?", and in the end take no action, or there was no action that could be taken, just wasted mental energy. Are you tired of being in that trap? Then it is time to de-clutter. From a kingdom perspective, we need to de-clutter to make ourselves more effective witnesses of the power of God. I would encourage you to read 2 Corinthians 4:4–7. Out of that passage, there are a couple of verses that really shine some light on this topic.

Verse 3 says, *"But if our gospel be hid, it is hid to them that are lost."* This answers the question of why we need to de-clutter. It can be a hindrance to our Christian witness. In the same chapter, verse 7 brings the point home when it says, *"But we have this treasure in earthen vessels, that the excellency of the power may be of God, and not of us."* We have inside us the Spirit of the living God, yet we allow it to be hidden by useless clutter in our hearts and lives. How is the lost world going to benefit from this treasure we possess if we don't put it on display? Back to my earlier example, all the items that were taken down didn't go back on the shelf or on the wall, only the best so that they could be clearly seen apart from the clutter.

How do we get rid of clutter in our heart? Much as we would with material clutter, we need to divide it up into piles, so to speak. Separate out the sin in your collection of clutter, for that is the most damaging and maybe the easiest to deal with. Repent of it, confess it to God, and ask for His help in overcoming. In the same manner, renounce your mental bad habits of worry and doubt and give them over to God for Him to help you resolve. In most cases, the past is the past, and nothing can be done to change it, but if there are situations in your life where you can go to some and make restitution, I encourage you to do so. Obviously, that would need to be foreshadowed in prayer, but with God by your side, it will work. Most of all, allow God to be at your side, and your de-cluttering will be a success.

The Turtle, the Opossum, and Abraham

I must admit that I do some of my best thinking while I am exercising, and when I say that, I mean riding my bike, or on a cold day, it means walking with so many clothes on some days that it is hard to move. I do not like to walk on a treadmill or go around in circles in a gym, but if those are for you, go for it. They are safer and more reliable means of exercise than mine, but I just do not like them. There is just something about being out in the fresh air and seeing different sights. The fresh air just clears my mind, I guess, and being out and alone helps me to focus.

Sometimes, it does not take much to get me started thinking, like the other day when I noticed a turtle on the side of the road. He was not moving; actually, he was flat, along with an opossum in much the same condition. The first thing I thought of was "you should learn from the mistakes of others and not end up like them." As my old friend Blaine always used to say, "There's no lesson like a bought lesson." But I'll add it is better to learn from one that someone else paid the price for.

Back to our friends the turtle and the opossum. Why did they end up as they did? The first thing we see is they were on the move, maybe not fast enough, maybe not in the right direction, but they weren't just sitting on the sidelines watching life go by. They gave it all they had, as long as they could. As we think about them, just picture in your mind how people must have thought about Abram. For in Genesis 12, starting in verse 1, it says, *"Now the LORD had said unto Abram, Get thee out of thy country, and from thy kindred, and from thy father's house, unto a land that I will shew thee,"* and continues in verse 2, *"and I will make of thee a great nation."*

It all comes down to where your faith is and what you are going to do with your life and effort.

Like my animal friends, Abram had an inward drive to move that no one else, besides his immediate family, I guess, knew anything about or would have understood. So, in much the same way as we wonder why animals move about and do the things they do, I'm sure Abram's neighbors wondered why he just packed up and moved. You say that Abram's travels worked out better than my turtle's did. And I would say you are right, but he didn't see that in the natural world. He saw it by faith in an all-powerful yet invisible God.

It all comes down to where your faith is and what you are going to do with your life and effort. God has a purpose and a plan for us all. Take him at his word and put your faith in action for whatever he has called you to do. You might end up like the turtle, but with God's help, you may end up as blessed as Abraham, after God changed his name and his life forever.

WELCOME
KEEP OUT!

The Least of These

As I travel, whether in a car or whatever means of transportation, I like to look around and see the sites. And if you asked my wife, she might say I look out in the fields more than on the road, but that's another story altogether. But let's get back to our subject for today. One day somewhere in the great U.S.A., I saw the most beautiful banner hanging from a garage. It was covered in birds of all kind and had "WELCOME" in big letters across the top. I thought that was great so warm and inviting. But, almost to my own disbelief, at the edge of the driveway was a sign that said "Keep Out."

I thought to myself, how could those two signs appear so close together? Then it crossed my mind how Jesus must feel when we lift up his name in praise on Sunday morning, while we turn our back on those in need all week long. In the twenty-fifth chapter of the gospel of Matthew, Jesus tells a story of people who did good works to the poor and needy, and He accepted it as if it was done unto him. Matthew 25:40 says, *"And the King shall answer and say unto them, Verily I say unto you, Inasmuch as ye have done it unto one of the least of these my brethren, ye have done it unto me."* I do not mean to condemn, just drawing our attention.

I know there are many of you that do many good works, which no one ever knows about it, and for that, you will be rewarded in heaven. But for the rest of us, I think that we need to try to do that in secret to bless others and make it more than our outward praise to Jesus for others to hear. James 3:11 says, *"Doth a fountain send forth at the same place sweet water and bitter?"* Let us let the words from our lips be sweet and full of praise. Moreover, let our actions speak louder than our words when we do good deeds for others, in Jesus' name. Above all, let us praise Jesus.

Look Ahead, Not Behind

Some time ago, I noticed a book review that caught my attention. I have not read the book nor am I endorsing the book, but the title caused me to think. The name of the book is *The Windshield's Bigger Than The Rearview Mirror,* and the author is Jeff Wickwire. So, I did a little research to put things into perspective. In comparison, the rearview mirror in my car is less than 2% the size of the windshield. So, using this for an example then, why do we spend so much time reflecting on the past deeds of our lives? If we spend too much time looking at the past, then it would be like driving your car down the road and only looking at the rearview mirror. I don't think that would be either safe of effective.

Paul said in Philippians 3:14; *"I press toward the mark for the prize of the high calling of God in Christ Jesus."* There comes a time when we have to let go of our past sins and mistakes and let God work in our lives and help us look forward, help us, as Paul suggests, to press toward the mark. Is there something holding you back today? This isn't something that I have myself conquered, as I seem to waste mental energy thinking about things and wondering if I handled a given situation correctly or if I should have done things differently. While it might help your future actions by learning from the mistakes of your past, you cannot dwell on them, for in most cases, there is nothing that can be changed. Forget the past, and press on to the future.

I encourage you to read the entire fourth chapter of the book of Philippians. For verse 6 says, *"Be careful for nothing; but in every thing by prayer and supplication with thanksgiving let your requests be made known unto God."* We all face things that in ourselves seem impossible, but if we turn to God, verse 13 says, *"I can do all things through Christ which strengtheneth me."* God loves to make the impossible possible. Is there something in your past that keeps your focus drawn away from your future? Turn it over to God and allow him full access into your life, make him Lord and Master. For in Philippians 4:19, Paul says, *"But my God shall supply all your need according to his riches in glory by Christ Jesus."* Claim that promise today for your life and your situation.

Retreat Doesn't Equal Surrender

I do not have to state the obvious that today we live in a fast-paced society. For most of us, that extends into all areas of our lives. Using myself as an example, I feel driven to do more and more and to go places when it seems there is no place left to go. As many of you have learned by now, I tend to preach to myself and hope it helps someone else, and this is another example of such teaching. Have you ever seen the bumper sticker that says something about driving faster than my guardian angel can fly? Well, while it in itself has no theological basis, let us apply the same thought to our walk with God.

Many times in my life, I have reached a point in some areas of life and in ministry where I felt things were at a standstill. Back to my example, the reality may have been that I was trying to go faster than God. Rather than following God or walking with God, I think maybe I have raced ahead and He made a left turn back at Albuquerque while I cruised on ahead, not noticing He turned. During those seasons, I have found that it is best to circle the wagons and slow down and get back in step with God, so to speak. Not by any means to stop but to still have that desire to serve Him, to seek Him and His direction.

God just expects us to do what He asks us to, no more no less.

A few years ago I got some serious inspiration from a road sign. The sign said "NO OUTLET." When you see a sign like that, do you go ahead and think you will find a way no one else sees? No, you proceed with caution, or maybe you go another way. A few minutes later, I felt the inspiration to say the words of my title, retreat doesn't equal surrender. As I meditated on that thought, I realized that retreat is actually a battle tactic. Putting the thoughts together, if you were a military commander and you saw no way of making forward progress, if you are in a valley and see a no outlet sign, rather than allowing your army to rush headlong into sure and certain destruction, you would have the bugler sound retreat. You're not giving up, just retiring to fight another day.

I realized, and what I want to share with you, is God only expects us to do what we can. He doesn't expect us to do more than we are able or to do everything that we want to do, even though we want to do it for Him. God just expects us to do what He asks us to, no more no less. And more importantly, God will enable and equip us to do His will. So what if He chooses to give us inspiration from a yellow road sign? Therefore, if you feel out of place today, quit walking around in circles and just sit and wait on God. Maybe you are just wearing yourself out when He just wants you to be sitting around resting while He makes things ready for your next move. He has a plan for you and in His time it will be revealed.

In Conclusion

"In conclusion…." That is what many preachers say just before they preach another 30 minutes. I say that in jest, but I have been on both sides of that coin. In the foreword I wrote of how difficult it is to begin something, and now I realize the challenges of bringing things to a close.

I guess it would be only logical for me to tell you that I have written this chapter last, but the reality is I am writing it as the layout is almost complete. With the flow of this book a little nontraditional, there wasn't a natural conclusion and we saw the need to include one more chapter. I toyed with the idea of titling it the final chapter, but for the reasons described I didn't.

It's not the final chapter, because I intend to write more books. Just the process of composing this book has taught me many lessons and has given me some great ideas and inspiration for my next book. I hope that you have enjoyed this book so much that you are looking forward to the next. But most importantly, it is my hope and prayer that you can apply the principles discussed within this book in your life, and not just your life, but that this book will encourage you to be a blessing and encouragement to others.

It's not the final chapter, because we all have more life to live and as long as we have breath the last chapter won't be written. But what if your life was to end before you finish this page? A song from several years ago comes to mind that asks an important question. Brian Free and Assurance had a song titled, "Where Would You be if Jesus Came Back 5 Minutes Ago?" I ask you today, what would be your answer to that question? Would you be in Heaven, or maybe somewhere less pleasant? No one wants to say Hell anymore, but it is a real place and will be filled with those who reject Christ's free gift of salvation. If you have never confessed Jesus as Lord and Master of your life, I beg you today to make that commitment.

Let's take that last question a step further. If you have accepted Christ as Savior, are you living a full life of joy and commitment to Christ? Do you walk through this life with the peace of God and the assurance of His love? Again, it is my hope and prayer that you can make practical application of the principles taught in this book to live a full life of inspiration and devotion and that the love of Christ is evident by everyone you meet.

As I have closed so many radio broadcast, I sincerely ask you to, "...believe the full gospel and live a full life."

Todd Hansen (Photo by Susan Jones of SKJ's Photo Box)

About the Author

Todd Hansen describes himself as a gospel singer. Is that how he earns a living? No, but that's who Todd is. One of the chapters of this book better defines that. Other words to describe Todd include author, songwriter, craftsman, and businessman.

Todd is a graduate of Murray State University with a Masters of Business Administration, and has many years in business management. The common thread in all these attributes is that Todd possesses a love for God and ministry, and has been reaching out in various forms for many years.

He previously produced a daily radio program on a local station and wrote a weekly devotional for a small chain of newspapers. Both of those ventures shared the name "Live a Full Life." Todd currently can be heard singing at area churches and at other local group settings such as nursing homes and Celebrate Recovery.

Todd and his wife Veronica are members of Salem Baptist Church in Salem, Kentucky. They have a "Brady Bunch" family consisting of three sons — Kyle, TJ, and Elijah — and three daughters — Ashley, Emily, and, yes, another Emily. All the children are grown and the number of grandchildren continues to grow....

Scriptural References

Scripture references appear bold,
page numbers appear italic.

Old Testament

Genesis
12:1 • *pp 92;* **45:5** • *pp 66*

Numbers
20:10 • *pp 80*

Deuteronomy
30:19 • *pp 71*

Joshua
Chapter 9 • *pp 45*

1 Samuel
30:6 • *pp 8*

1 Kings
Chapter 18 • *pp 24;* **19** • *pp 23;* **19:7–16** • *pp 26;* **19:18** • *pp 26*

Proverbs
3:5-6 • *pp 60*

Isaiah
53:5 • *pp 49*

New Testament

Matthew
5:10 • *pp 27;* **5: 16** • *pp 27;* **17:21** • *pp 51;* **25:40** • *pp 95*

Mark
6:34 • *pp 21*

John
10:10 • *pp 71*

Acts
Chapter 14 • *pp 83*

Romans
10:14 • *pp 21*

1 Corinthians
6:12 • *pp 80;* **12:7** • *pp 68*

2 Corinthians

4:3 • *pp 89;* **4:4–7** • *pp 89;* **4:7** • *pp 90;* **11:25** • *pp 83;* **12:2** • *pp 83;* **12:4** • *pp 83*

Ephesians

4:31 • *pp 87*

Philippians

3:7–8 • *pp 36;* **3:14** • *pp 97;* **4:6** • *pp 98;* **4:13** • *pp 98;* **4:19** • *pp 98*

James

1:21 • *pp 87;* **3:11** • *pp 96;* **4:2** • *pp 53;* **5:16** • *pp 52*

1 Peter

5:8 • *pp 39;* **5:9** • *pp 40*

Biblical Characters & Terms

A

Aaron 80
Abraham 66, 93
Abram 92

B

Baal 24, 25, 26

C

Canaan 41, 42, 43, 45, 46
Christ 27, 30, 31, 36, 38, 69, 72, 83, 97, 98, 104

D

David 8

E

Egypt 19, 41, 42, 43, 44
Elijah 23, 24, 25
Eve 80

G

Gibeon 45
Gibeonites 45, 47
God 16, 17, 19, 20, 21, 23, 24, 25, 26, 29, 30, 31, 32, 33, 36, 38, 40, 41, 42, 43, 44, 45, 46, 47, 48, 49, 50, 52, 53, 54, 55, 56, 57, 60, 61, 62, 63, 64, 65, 66, 68, 70, 72, 77, 79, 80, 81, 82, 87, 90, 97, 98, 99, 100

H

Holy Spirit 87

I

Isaiah 50
Israel 26
Israelites 41, 42, 43

J

James 74
Jesus 37, 50, 51, 71, 72, 78, 95, 96, 104
Jezebel 25
John 68
Joseph 41, 42, 43, 65, 66
Joshua 45, 46, 47

L

Lot 42
Luke 68

M

Mark 68
Mary 68
Moses 71, 80

P

Paul 36, 51, 68, 69, 80, 83, 85, 97
Peter 39, 44, 68
Promised Land 80

S

Satan 26, 40, 44, 72, 79

INDEX

A

Alamo, The 73

B

Brian Free and Assurance 104

C

Carroll, McGruder 51
Celebrate Recovery 107

D

Don't Ever Sell Your Saddle 29

E

Easter, Jeff 36
Easter, Sheri 36
Elliott Ford 33
Evans, Dr. Tony 51

G

Graham, Billy 28

H

Hansen, Juanita 10
Hansen, JW 10
Hansen, Mary Lue 10
Hansen, Max 10, 85
Hansen, Todd 106, 107
Hansen, Veronica 87, 107

J

Jesus Take the Wheel 30

L

Lincoln, Abraham 65, 66

M

McGruder, Priscilla 51
Mt. Pleasant, Texas 33
Murray State University 107

P

Paducah, Kentucky 39

S

Salem Baptist Church 107
Salem, Kentucky 107
Sea World 73

T

The Urban Alternative 51
The Windshield's Bigger Than The Rearview Mirror 97
Travis, Randy 29
Tribble, Kim 29

U

Underwood, Carrie 30

W

Wayne, John 24
Where Would You be if Jesus Came Back 5 Minutes Ago? 104
Wickwire, Jeff 97